THE
MAGNIFICENT
BOOK OF TREASURES
VIKINGS

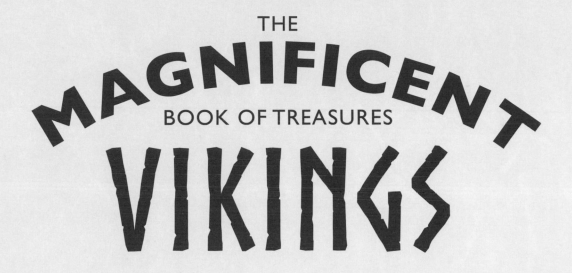

THE
MAGNIFICENT
BOOK OF TREASURES
VIKINGS

ILLUSTRATED BY EUGENIA NOBATI
WRITTEN BY STELLA CALDWELL

weldon**owen**

Written by Stella Caldwell
Illustrated by Eugenia Nobati
Consultant: Dr. Steve Ashby

weldon**owen**

Published by Weldon Owen Children's Books
An imprint of Weldon Owen International, L.P.
A subsidiary of Insight International, L.P.
PO Box 3088
San Rafael, CA 94912
www.insighteditions.com

Designer: Karen Wilks
Editor: George Maudsley
Senior Production Manager: Greg Steffen

Art Director: Stuart Smith
Publisher: Sue Grabham

CEO: Raoul Goff

ISBN: 978-1-68188-902-3

Manufactured and printed in China
First printing, April 2023 TOP0423
27 26 25 24 23 5 4 3 2 1

INTRODUCTION

More than a thousand years ago, the Vikings set sail from Scandinavia in search of glory and new lands. They were fearless warriors and daring explorers who ventured far and wide. But they were also wonderful storytellers, skilled traders, and superb craftspeople. Woodworkers built fast, sleek ships, metalworkers crafted spectacular jewelry and ornate weapons, and weavers made fine clothes.

The Magnificent Book of Treasures Vikings takes you on a thrilling voyage to discover this great seafaring people. Wonder at a beautiful longship and imagine what it was like to navigate it through wild and stormy seas. Meet fierce warriors, mythical beasts, and noble kings such as Gorm the Old. Learn about Odin, the mighty king of the gods, the fertility goddess Freya, and the flying warrior women called Valkyries.

Read about how ordinary Viking families lived, and see an antler comb and a child's wooden toy. Find out why wealthy Vikings were buried with precious jewelry, prized weapons, and ordinary household objects. Marvel at Thor's magic hammer, an intricately carved dragon head, and a perfectly preserved leather boot.

Travel back in time to discover some of the most magnificent Viking treasures ever found.

FACT FILE

Discovered: Oseberg burial mound, near Tønsberg, Norway

Found today: Viking Ship Museum, Oslo, Norway

Date: About 820 CE

Materials: Maple wood

Size: 20 in (50 cm) long

⚜ CONTENTS ⚜

SHIP OF THE DEAD

- Wealthy and important Vikings were sometimes buried in ships. The Vikings believed these would carry them safely to the afterlife. This ship contained the bones of two women, along with prized belongings including clothes, sleighs, furniture, tapestries, and kitchen equipment.

- This ship was found in a burial mound. Although the mound's soggy clay stopped the ship's wood from rotting away, the weight of the soil and stones broke it into thousands of pieces. It took experts many years to carefully put it back together again.

- Animal carvings decorate both ends of this ship. The front displays a serpent's spiraling head, while the back forms its twisting tail. The Vikings often mounted the carved heads of snakes or dragons on their ships to frighten their enemies.

- This ship had room for 30 oarsmen. Fifteen pairs of oars were found inside, but they showed little sign of use. Perhaps they were made for the burial of the women found in this boat.

FACT FILE

Discovered: Oseberg burial mound, near Tønsberg, Norway

Found today: Viking Ship Museum, Oslo, Norway

Date: 820 CE

Materials: Oak, pine

Size: 70½ ft (21.5 m) long

The long pole is the ship's mast. Attached to it was a sail. This allowed Vikings to travel far across the open sea. When there was no wind, or in coastal waters and rivers, they dropped the mast and rowed.

Sometimes animals and even servants were sacrificed and buried alongside their Viking owners. The remains of 15 horses, six dogs, and two cows were found in this ship.

The Vikings were skilled shipbuilders and sailors. Their light, wooden longships carried warriors, traders, and explorers swiftly across the seas. This longship is one of the best-preserved Viking discoveries ever made.

THE GREAT WOLF

- This rune stone is a memorial to a man named Ulfr. His name means "wolf" in Old Norse. Ulfr's family wanted to remember him as a fierce and brave warrior.

- A serpent carved with runes coils around the edge of this stone. There were 16 basic letters in the runic alphabet. Each letter was made of straight or diagonal lines.

- It is thought these pictures of a wolf and a ship are part of the Ragnarök myth. Ragnarök means "doom of the gods." The Vikings believed that the giant wolf Fenrir would gobble up the god Odin at this dreadful event.

- The importance of ancient rune stones was not always understood. After Viking times, they were sometimes used to build walls and roads. This rune stone was discovered 400 years ago in the wall of an old church.

- The ship on this stone is thought to be a horrifying vessel called *Naglfar*. In myths, it was made from the toenails and fingernails of the dead. The Vikings believed it would carry monsters to join the final battle against the gods.

- The circles along the top of the boat represent warriors' round shields. Viking shields were made of wood with a round iron "boss" at the center. On the back of the boss was a handle for holding the shield.

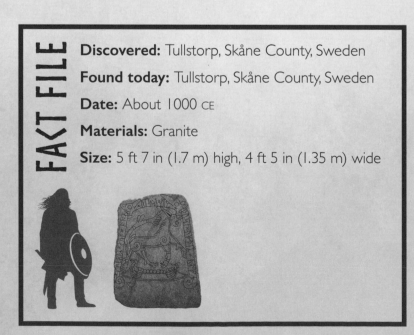

FACT FILE

Discovered: Tullstorp, Skåne County, Sweden

Found today: Tullstorp, Skåne County, Sweden

Date: About 1000 CE

Materials: Granite

Size: 5 ft 7 in (1.7 m) high, 4 ft 5 in (1.35 m) wide

THE HAMMER OF THOR

- This little pendant represents the enchanted hammer of the god of thunder, Thor. The Vikings told many stories about Thor's battles with giants, trolls, and serpents. His powerful hammer could crush monsters and flatten mountains.

- The Vikings believed that many gods and goddesses ruled the universe. Thor was one of the most important gods, and one of the strongest.

- Two dwarf brothers made the hammer for Thor. The mischievous god Loki disguised himself as a fly and buzzed around their heads while they worked. Distracted by the buzzing, they made the hammer with too short a handle.

- The gold and silver on this pendant were not mined locally. Jewelers had to acquire these precious metals by melting down coins and treasures from other lands. They were often objects that had been stolen during Viking raids.

- This pendant was worn as a lucky charm on a necklace. The owner might have prayed for Thor's protection in battle, or while sailing on rough and stormy seas.

- Thor's hammer was called Mjölnir, which means lightning. The Vikings believed that lightning was caused by Thor hurling his hammer toward Earth. The hammer always returned to him, like a boomerang.

FAKT FILE

Discovered: Ödeshög, Östergötland, Sweden

Found today: Swedish History Museum, Stockholm, Sweden

Date: 900–1000 CE

Materials: Gold, silver

Size: 2½ in (6.5 cm) high, 1½ in (4 cm) wide

13

A WARRIOR'S HELMET

- A rich and powerful warrior wore this helmet in battle. It was lined with wool or leather to protect the warrior's head from injury. The iron frame guarded the eyes and nose, while plates at the back protected the neck.

- This helmet is one of only two that have survived from the Viking age. It was found in a grave in nine fragments and needed to be reconstructed.

- Viking warriors did not wear a uniform. They dressed and armed themselves. As well as a helmet, they wore a padded leather tunic or a chain mail shirt to protect their body. They carried a round, wooden shield to ward off blows from sharp spears, swords, and arrows.

- Only the wealthiest Vikings wore iron helmets, which is why so few have been discovered. Most warriors may have worn a cap made of hard leather.

- Many other treasures were discovered alongside this helmet. These included a chain mail shirt, weapons, dice and game pieces, a sledge, and stirrups. The Vikings believed a dead warrior would need these things in the next world.

- Vikings are sometimes shown wearing horned helmets. This idea is a myth, however, as no such helmets have ever been found.

FACT FILE

Discovered: Gjermundbu farm, near Haugsbygd, Norway

Found today: Museum of Cultural History, Oslo, Norway

Date: 950–1000 CE

Materials: Iron

Size: 8¼ in (21 cm) wide

THE GREAT PROCESSION

- A procession of horses and people moves from right to left across this lively scene. You can see houses and a ship with six people inside. This wall hanging, or tapestry, is one of the oldest textiles ever found.

- This tapestry is one of five discovered together. They are decorated with a mixture of Christian and Norse symbols.

- Many archaeologists think this tapestry shows Ragnarök, the great battle between good and evil at the end of the world. Gods would fight monsters, and almost everything in the universe would be destroyed.

- A weaver made this tapestry on a loom. Some parts are more even than others. This might mean that more than one weaver helped to create it.

- An artist found the tapestry in 1909 on the dusty floor of a shed next to an old church. After it had been cleaned, experts realized the importance of the find.

- The large tree probably represents Yggdrasil. The Vikings believed this great ash tree supported the nine realms of the universe. A cruel dragon called Nidhogg gnawed at Yggdrasil's roots from below.

- The tapestry's colors were once bright. They were made using vegetable dye. The blue came from the woad plant, the red from madder roots, and the yellow from the weld plant.

17

WOODEN WAGON

- This beautiful wagon was discovered in a famous burial ship in Oseberg, Norway. Its solid wooden wheels would not have been suitable for long distances. It was probably used in a religious ceremony. Or perhaps it was for a funeral procession or to transport a wealthy woman to and from a ship.

- This is the only complete wagon known from Viking times. It could be taken apart, perhaps to be carried on a ship.

- The carvings show scenes from Viking myths. On the front you can see a man being attacked by writhing snakes. This is probably Gunnar, who was thrown into a snake pit because he refused to say where he had hidden a treasure hoard.

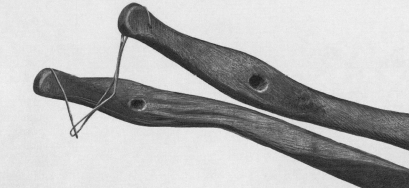

FACT FILE

Discovered: Oseberg burial mound, near Tønsberg, Norway

Found today: Viking Ship Museum, Oslo, Norway

Date: Around 834 CE

Materials: Oak, ash, iron

Size: 18 ft (5.5 m) long, 5 ft (1.5 m) wide, 4 ft (1.2 m) high

Several cats and a woman are carved on the far end of the wagon. They are thought to represent the goddess of fertility, Freya. She drove a chariot pulled by two cats.

The heads of four bearded men decorate the wagon. Viking men were sometimes named after their beards. The first Viking king to rule over England was called Sweyn Forkbeard.

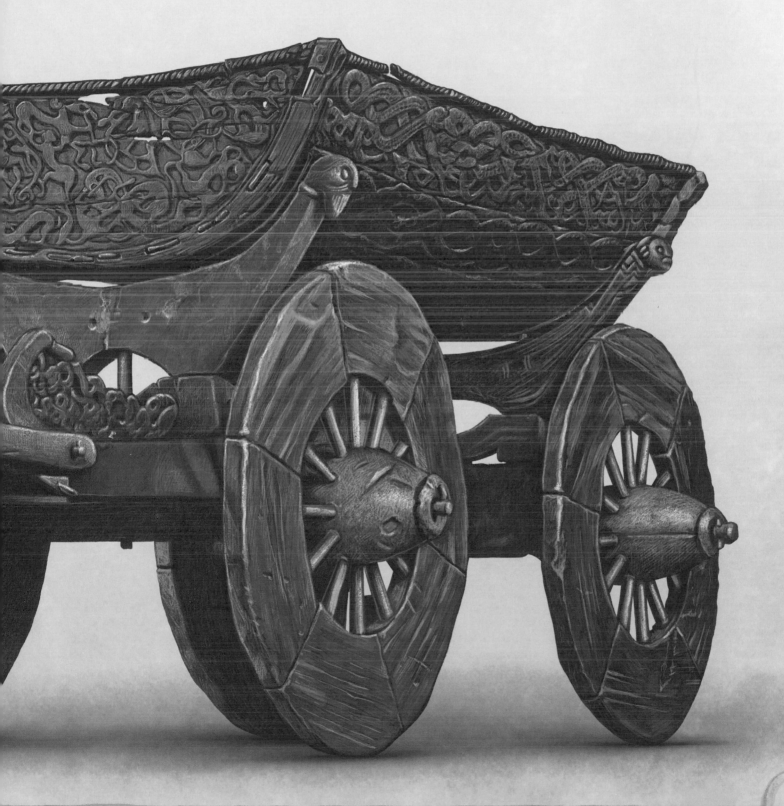

VALKYRIE WARRIOR

- This little figurine is the size of your thumb. Some experts think it shows a female warrior called a Valkyrie.

- In Viking myths, Valkyries gathered the souls of slain warriors from the battlefield. They carried the warriors back to the great hall Valhalla, where the god Odin welcomed them.

- The figure is armed with a short sword and a round shield for protection from enemy blows.

- The warrior's lower legs and feet are missing. Someone could have begun to chop the figure up to melt the pieces for new valuable jewelry.

- The woman's hair is twisted into a ponytail. A hole at the back of her neck shows that someone wore this figure on a chain.

- A number of Valkyrie figures have been discovered, but they have all been flat. This figure is rounded and three-dimensional.

- In some legends, Valkyries rode to the battlefield on horseback. In others, they flew swiftly across the sky using their magic cloaks.

- The figure wears a long, patterned dress. Viking women usually wore an ankle-length "under-dress" covered by a shorter "over-dress." The over-dress had straps like an apron, which were held in place by two brooches.

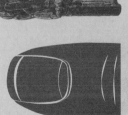

FACT FILE

Discovered: Hårby, Denmark

Found today: National Museum of Denmark, Copenhagen, Denmark

Date: About 800 CE

Materials: Silver, black nello

Size: 1¼ in (3.4 cm) high

A GIFT FOR A QUEEN

- This beautiful casket belonged to a German queen called Kunigunde. She was married to Henry II, the Holy Roman emperor. Viking travelers from Denmark probably brought the box to Germany as a special gift for the royal couple.

- There is a Christian cross on this casket, as well as symbols from Viking legends. Many objects from this period show scenes from the Bible as well as from Viking myths.

- The casket was probably used as a jewelry box. It was a grand item that showed the owner's wealth and importance.

- The oak box is covered with thin sheets of carved ivory from the tusks of a walrus. The Vikings hunted walrus in Greenland and the Arctic north for their skins and precious ivory. The skins could be turned into rope and the ivory sold for carving.

- The Vikings often decorated their tools, weapons, and jewelry with real and imaginary animals. You can see the shapes of strange creatures in the swirling patterns on this box.

FACT FILE

Discovered: Bamberg, Germany

Found today: Bavarian National Museum, Munich, Germany

Date: About 1000 CE

Materials: Oak, ivory, bronze, iron, rock crystal

Size: 5¼ in (13.3 cm) high

The style of art on this casket is called the Mammen style. It is named after a famous decorated axe, which was found in Mammen, Denmark. This style used animals and birds as well as swirling plants and leaves in its designs.

DECORATED SPOON

- This patterned spoon is carved from deer antler. The Vikings used different types of animal bone to make objects. Archaeologists have found combs, musical instruments, dice, and ice skates made from bone.

- Spoons, knives, and fingers were used for eating food. The Vikings did not have forks. Food was probably chopped up before it was cooked to make it easier to eat.

- Vikings would have eaten a lot of meat and fish, as well as cabbage and green vegetables, such as leeks. Often these were cooked in pots, like the stews eaten today.

- Spoons were usually made from bone or wood. Wealthier people might own spoons made from more expensive materials, such as copper or silver.

The antler used by the Vikings usually came from red deer. In northern Scandinavia, reindeer and elk antlers were also used.

Most Vikings were farmers, so bones from animals such as cattle, sheep, and horses were widely available. Bone objects were cheap to make and did not usually need a skilled craftperson, unless they were highly decorated like this spoon.

Whale bone was used for special objects, such as flat boards to smooth out wrinkles in clothing. The Vikings sometimes hunted whales, but this was very dangerous. Whale bone was often taken from creatures that had been washed ashore.

FACT FILE

Discovered: Björkö, Adelsö, Uppland, Sweden

Found today: Swedish History Museum, Stockholm, Sweden

Date: 793–1100 CE

Materials: Deer antler

Size: 5½ in (14 cm) long, 1½ in (3.9 cm) wide

THE AMBER KING

- This intricately carved amber figure was used as a piece in a board game.

- The game piece may have represented the king in the popular Viking game *hneftafl*. The game was played on a wooden board. One player used their 16 pieces to capture the king from the other player, who had eight pieces.

- Some experts think the game piece symbolizes the Viking god of growth and fertility, Frey. His twin sister was the goddess of fertility, Freya. People asked Frey to bless their marriages and to give them healthy children. In the spring, farmers prayed to Frey for a rich harvest.

- This object is made from amber, which is the fossilized resin of pine trees. The Vikings treasured this bright, red-golden material, and also used it to make beads, pendants, and amulets.

- The game piece is a carving of a man holding his long beard. Viking men took pride in their appearance and kept themselves well groomed.

- Not all board games were played with expensive game pieces. Less wealthy Vikings used simple counters made from broken pottery or bone. A game board could be scratched onto wood or stone.

FACT FILE

Discovered: Roholte, Denmark

Found today: National Museum of Denmark, Copenhagen, Denmark

Date: 900–1100 CE

Materials: Amber

Size: Approx. 2 in (5 cm) high

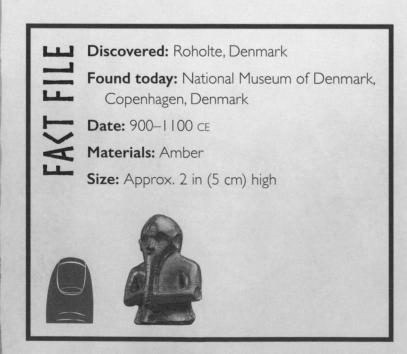

BRONZE WEATHER VANE

- This glinting weather vane hung from the front of a Viking ship. It showed the sailors which direction the wind was blowing from. The lion on top always pointed away from the wind.

- The Vikings were brilliant sailors. They did not have charts or compasses to help them find their way across stormy seas. Instead, they looked at the position of the Sun, Moon, and stars, and relied on their knowledge of wind patterns and sea life to help them reach distant lands.

- Wind and rain have damaged the vane, and the metal is dented in places from years of use.

- A winged dragon decorates the vane. In Viking myths, dragons were fierce symbols of strength and destruction.

- The dragon shown on this vane fights with a wolf and a serpent. On the left, the wolf's jaws clamp around the dragon's leg, while further right the long serpent coils around the dragon's body.

FACT FILE

Discovered: Söderala, Sweden

Found today: Swedish History Museum, Stockholm, Sweden

Date: 1050 CE

Materials: Gilded bronze

Size: 9 in (23 cm) high, 13½ in (34.5 cm) wide

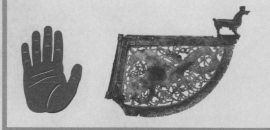

The vane was found on a Swedish church spire, but experts are not sure where it was made. Some of its details are similar to Viking objects from Sweden, yet the dragon's head and wings look similar to Viking art made in Britain and Ireland.

MARKER FOR THE DEAD

- In Scandinavia, it was rare for the Vikings to mark their graves with tombstones. But this stone was found in England, where tombstones were commonplace. As the Vikings traveled to new places, they began to take on the customs and beliefs of the people around them.

- The style of art on the stone is called the Ringerike style. It features mythical beasts and swirling plants and leaves. The Ringerike style is hardly ever found outside Scandinavia, which makes this discovery very unusual.

- This tombstone was made by a master stonemason, and probably marks the grave of an important Scandinavian buried in London.

- The runes on the side of the stone say that "Ginna and Toki had this stone laid." The person buried in the tomb was probably the husband of Ginna and the father of Toki.

- Some archaeologists believe this carving shows a lion and a serpent. Others think it is the god Odin's eight-legged horse, Sleipnir. But most experts think the creature is a mix of several different beasts from Viking legends.

- Traces of red, white, and black paint were found on the stone. This tells us that the tombstone was painted in bright colors at the time of the burial.

FAKT FILE

Discovered: St Paul's Cathedral, London, UK

Found today: Museum of London, London, UK

Date: About 1030 CE

Materials: Limestone, paint

Size: 18½ in (47 cm) high, 22½ in (57 cm) wide, 4 in (10 cm) deep

THE GOD OF THUNDER

- The warrior god Thor sits on his throne. Thor was an immensely strong god with long hair and a bushy beard. The Vikings prayed for his protection in battle and wild storms.

- Thor was the god of thunder and lightning. He traveled across the sky in a great chariot pulled by two goats. The Vikings believed the crash of thunder was the roar of his chariot wheels.

- Thor clutches his magical hammer in his hands. He would hurl this deadly weapon at his enemies. Thor also used his hammer to bless marriages and births.

- The English word Thursday is named after Thor. In Old English, Thursday means "Thor's day."

- The Vikings believed the most important gods and goddesses lived in a part of the universe called Asgard. It was Thor's job to protect Asgard from giants and other terrifying monsters.

- Thor wore iron gloves and had an enchanted belt. These magical possessions helped him to double his strength.

This statue was discovered in Iceland. The first Viking settlers arrived on this remote island more than a thousand years ago.

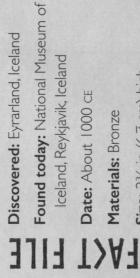

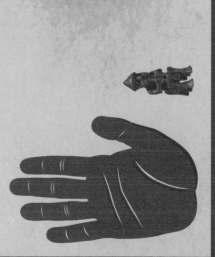

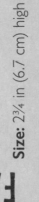

CHRISTIAN CRUCIFIX

- This cross is made of solid gold. The small loop at the top shows that it was part of a necklace. A wealthy Viking would have proudly worn it on a chain or a string of beads.

- Christ on the cross is a powerful symbol of the Christian religion. This crucifix is the oldest example ever discovered in Denmark. It was made at a time when Christianity was beginning to replace the old Viking religion.

- The cross was found after scanning a field with a metal detector. Its Viking owner might have been out walking when they lost the prized pendant.

- The craftsperson who made this cross was very skilled. The front is made from fine gold threads and beads. The back of the cross is smooth and flat.

- It was once thought that a famous rune stone built by the Danish king Harald Bluetooth showed the oldest image of Christ in Scandinavia. But archaeologists think that this gold crucifix might be even older.

- This object is very similar to a silver cross discovered in Birka, Sweden. That cross was found buried in the grave of a Viking woman. It is possible both were made by the same person.

FACT FILE

Discovered: Aunslev, Denmark

Found today: Viking Museum Ladby, Kerteminde, Denmark

Date: About 900–950 CE

Materials: Gold

Size: 1½ in (4 cm) high

ANTLER COMBS

FACT FILE

Discovered: Björkö, Adelsö, Uppland, Sweden

Found today: Swedish History Museum, Stockholm, Sweden

Date: 800–1100 CE

Materials: Deer antler; iron

Size: Approx. 1¼ in (3.2 cm) high, 5¼ in (13.5 cm) long

- The Vikings liked to keep their hair well groomed. Both men and women used combs to smooth their hair and remove dirt.

- Unmarried women often combed their long hair so it hung loose, or wore it in braids. Married women usually gathered their hair into a bun at the back of the neck, or kept it in a headdress that was tied under the chin.

- These combs have two antler plates at the top. The spiked teeth of the combs have been fixed between the plates with iron rivets.

- Viking men often wore their hair short at the back and long at the front. An English letter from around 995 CE describes how Danish Vikings were blinded by their long fringes!

- Warriors often carried combs, as well as swords and knives, on their belts.

- The Vikings took great care over their appearance. As well as combing their hair, they regularly washed their hair, bodies, and hands. Unwanted hairs could be plucked with metal tweezers, and metal picks were used to clean nails.

- It took a craftsperson about two days to make a comb. Some were carved with a pattern, design or rune letters, or with metal rivets and plating.

- Many Vikings were buried with their combs. Sometimes the combs had a special case to protect their delicate teeth. These things show us that the comb was a valued object that was expected to last a lifetime.

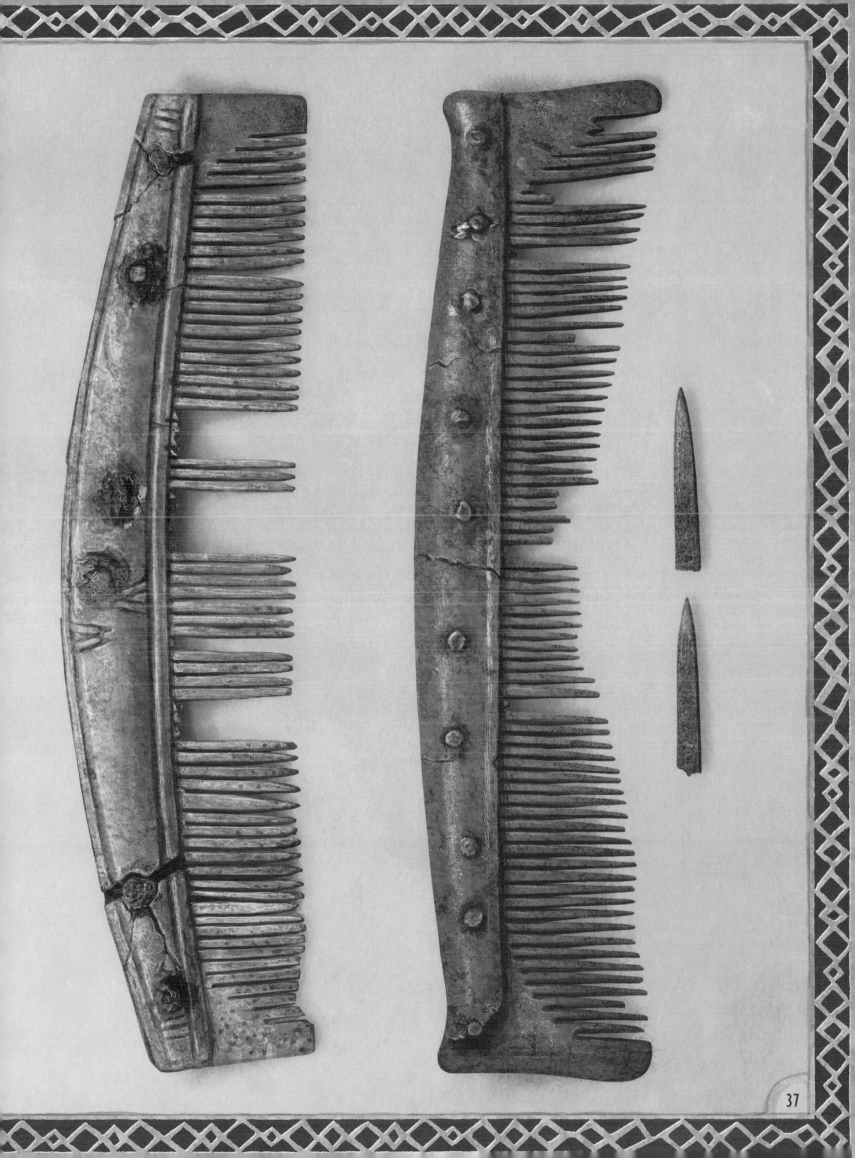

A CHILD'S TOY

- Around 950 years ago, a child living in Norway had fun playing with this little wooden horse. Its simple shape was carved from a flat piece of wood.

- Horses were important to the Vikings for riding and for pulling sledges and wagons. Vikings were often buried with their riding equipment, such as stirrups or saddles. Some people were even buried with their horses.

- Viking children didn't just play with toys. From a young age, they helped to clean, cook, and make clothes. Outside, they worked hard in the fields, gathered firewood, and helped with the family's animals.

- Children's graves have been discovered containing miniature objects, such as an axe and a spear. Perhaps they were favorite toys. Or maybe they were objects used to teach adult skills, such as fighting.

- Archaeologists have discovered other wooden toys from the Viking age, including simple dolls, ships, and animals.

- The Víga-Glúms saga is a Viking story set in Iceland. In one scene, it describes how a young boy of six thinks he is too old for his bronze toy horse. He decides a younger child would enjoy it more and gives it away.

FAKT FILE

Discovered: Trondheim, Norway

Found today: NTNU University Museum, Trondheim, Norway

Date: About 1075 CE

Materials: Wood

Size: 5 in (12.7 cm) long

STONE DRAGON

- A Viking metalworker used this mold to make dragon-shaped clothespins. They heated metal, such as silver or lead, over a fire. Then they poured the melted metal into the mold and waited for it to cool and harden.

- A mold such as this one could be used again and again. The dress pins made with it were used to fasten clothes at the collar or the waist. They were also worn as a striking decoration.

- The dragon's gaping jaws are lined with pointed teeth. It has a horn on its forehead and a long, curly mane. The creature resembles the carved dragon heads that decorated the front of Viking longships.

- This mold is made of soapstone, which is soft and easy to carve. The Vikings also used soapstone to make objects such as cooking pots.

- The mold was discovered in the Swedish town of Birka, which was once a very important trading center. People traveled from far and wide to buy and sell things there. Viking craftspeople and jewelers set up workshops in Birka and sold their goods at the markets.

FACT FILE

Discovered: Birka, Sweden

Found today: Swedish History Museum, Stockholm, Sweden

Date: About 850 CE

Materials: Soapstone

Size: 3¼ in (8.1 cm) high, 2½ in (6.6 cm) wide

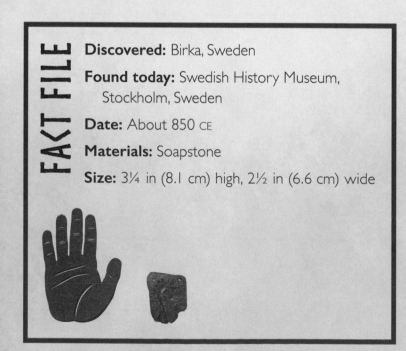

THE SNARLING BEAST

◈ The mysterious creature on this wooden post shows the incredible skill of Viking woodcarvers. It would have taken the artist a long time to shape the wood and then carve such exquisite details.

◈ Some experts think the head is of an animal, such as a dog or bear. Others believe it is a mythical creature, perhaps the sea serpent Jörmungandr. The Vikings believed this monster could crush ships in its huge jaws.

◈ Four other posts topped by mysterious animal heads were discovered alongside this one. It is thought they were each made by different woodcarvers.

◈ Perhaps this fierce animal was meant to scare away evil spirits. The post may have decorated a house or a throne, or it could have been used as part of a religious ceremony.

◈ The Vikings used a lot of swirling patterns on their art and crafts. The style of pattern used on this post is known as Oseberg, named after the burial ship on which the carving was found.

The post is made from hard maple wood, which is not easy to carve. The artist probably used a carving knife, a file, and a tool called a rasp to shape the head.

The wood used to make this carving was widely available in Scandinavia and was an important material for the Vikings. It was used to build houses and ships, and to make everyday objects such as shields, furniture, looms, and eating utensils.

FACT FILE

Discovered: Oseberg burial mound, near Tønsberg, Norway

Found today: Viking Ship Museum, Oslo, Norway

Date: About 820 CE

Materials: Maple wood

Size: 19¾ in (50 cm) high

THE UNKNOWN VIKING

🛡 This male face is full of character, but nobody knows who he is. While the Vikings wrote messages on stones and wood, they did not write books. That is why it can be hard to find out who the people in Viking art are.

🛡 This silver head was worn as a pendant on a chain. You can see the loop for the chain at the top. It was probably a good luck charm, or could have been meant to frighten enemies.

🛡 A bird decorates the man's helmet. Its beak points downward at his nose, while its wings stretch down either side of the helmet.

🛡 Important Vikings were celebrated in art. Only rich and powerful chieftains wore metal helmets, so perhaps the face of this helmeted man belongs to a heroic warrior. Or maybe it is instead that of a Viking god.

🛡 The pendant was discovered in a rich woman's grave. The Vikings buried their dead with weapons, jewelry, and other grave goods, although this may not have been true for the poorest people.

FACT FILE

Discovered: Aska, Östergötland, Sweden

Found today: Swedish History Museum, Stockholm, Sweden

Date: 800–1100 CE

Materials: Silver

Size: Approx. 1¼ in (3.1 cm) high, ¾ in (1.6 cm) wide

Viking traders often used silver as a way of paying for goods. They could chop up jewelry like this pendant and use the silver pieces like money. This was known as hack silver.

A CHIEFTAIN'S BRAID

- This richly embroidered piece of silk was discovered in a chieftain's grave. It is the end of a long braid that was probably used to fasten a cloak at the neck. The braid would have hung down the chieftain's front.

- A tunic and a fur-lined cloak were discovered with this braid. They were in poor condition but were once splendid clothes decorated with leopards, birds, leaves, and human faces.

- The braid was made by a specialist. Its brown silk has gold embroidery around the edges. The expensive materials show the owner was wealthy and had an important place in Viking society.

- It was the job of women to make clothes for their families. Most people's clothes were made from wool, linen, or animal skins. A spindle was used to create thread, and a loom was used to weave the thread into cloth.

- As well as a cloak, most Viking men wore woollen trousers and a long woollen tunic. They used buckles and brooches as fasteners.

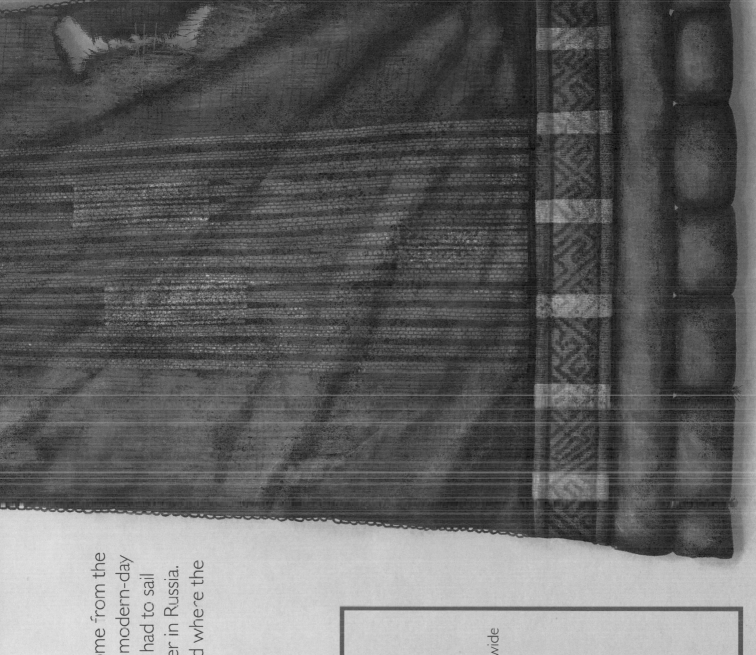

The silk for this braid may have come from the faraway city of Constantinople, in modern-day Turkey. To reach it, Viking traders had to sail their boats along the Dnieper River in Russia. They pulled their boats across land where the river was fast and dangerous.

FACT FILE

Discovered: Mammen, Denmark

Found today: National Museum of Denmark, Copenhagen, Denmark

Date: 970–971 CE

Materials: Silk, gold thread

Size: 8 in (20.2 cm) long, 3 in (7.5 cm) wide

NECKLACE OF FISH TAILS

- The Vikings loved to wear bright, eye-catching jewelry. This necklace has 110 glass beads and 19 bronze pendants in the shape of fish tails.

- Glass was not made in Scandinavia. Viking traders brought it back from western Europe as well as from eastern cities such as Istanbul and Jerusalem. Sometimes they brought broken glass vessels that could be melted down to make other objects, such as these beads.

- Glass beads were usually worn by women. This necklace was discovered in a woman's grave and must have been a treasured possession.

- To make beads, glass was heated in a furnace. The beads were shaped using a special rod called a mandrel. Different-colored glass could be fused together to make multicolored beads, and patterns could be added after the bead was made.

FACT FILE

Discovered: Norrkvie, Grötlingbo Parish, Gotland, Sweden

Found today: Swedish History Museum, Stockholm, Sweden

Date: 800–1100 CE

Materials: Glass, bronze

Size: 9 in (23 cm) wide, 5¾ in (14.5 cm) high

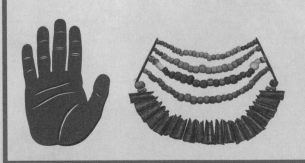

This necklace was discovered on the island of Gotland, in the Baltic Sea. In Gotland, beads were sometimes made from fossilized sea lilies and corals. White beads could be made from seashells such as cowrie shells.

RING OF CHARMS

- Five gleaming amulets, or lucky charms, hang from this silver ring. An expert cleaned the object after it was found to make it shine as it did in Viking times.

- These charms were probably carried for protection and to bring good fortune. A warrior might have hoped they would give strength in battle. Or perhaps a trader prayed they would bring a safe and profitable journey.

- The little charm on the left is a steel fire starter. In Viking times, fires were made by striking steel against flint to create a spark.

- The large charm at the bottom is a miniature sword. For the Vikings, the sword was an important symbol of power, strength, and bravery.

- Viking craftspeople made many miniature objects like these charms, including weapons, animals, and even furniture. They could be worn around the neck as pendants or attached to clothes as brooches or pins.

- The three straight charms could represent the magical wands of women called *völvas*. The Vikings believed these women were witches who had the ability to see the future. The Old Norse word *völva* means "wand carrier."

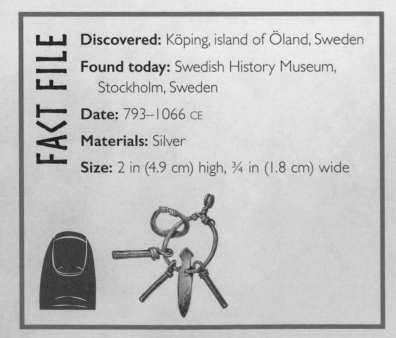

FACT FILE

Discovered: Köping, island of Öland, Sweden

Found today: Swedish History Museum, Stockholm, Sweden

Date: 793–1066 CE

Materials: Silver

Size: 2 in (4.9 cm) high, ¾ in (1.8 cm) wide

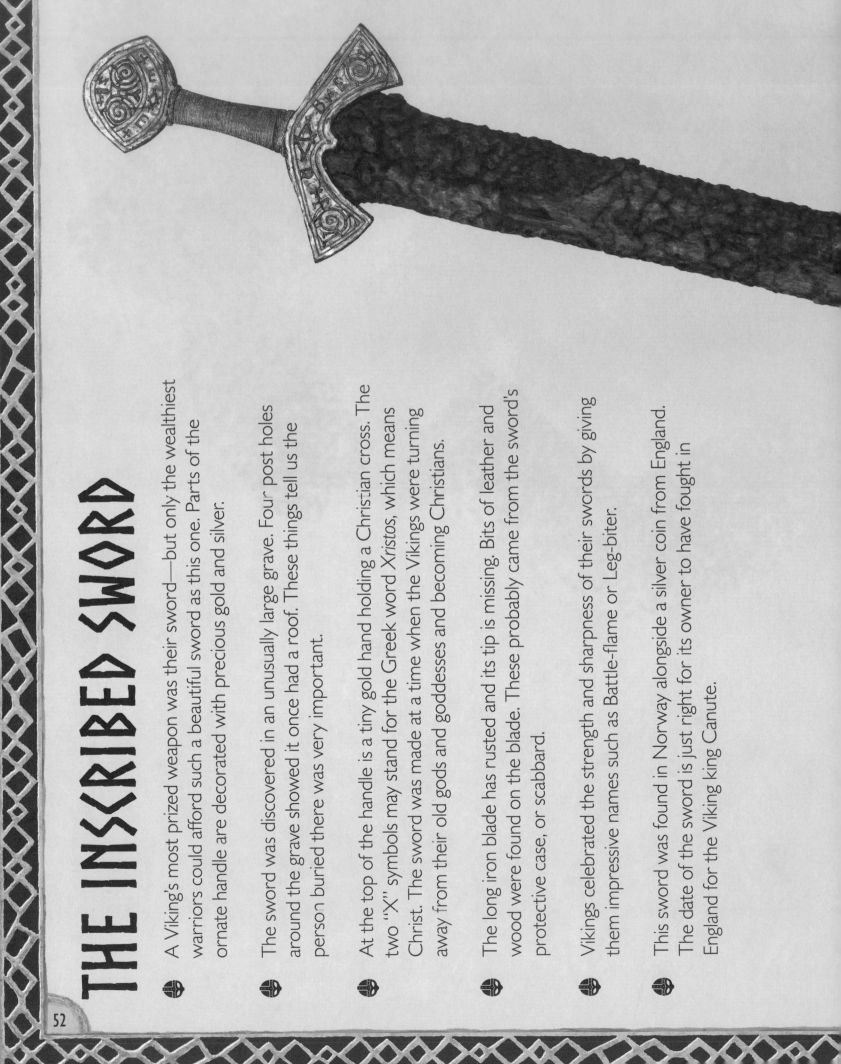

THE INSCRIBED SWORD

- A Viking's most prized weapon was their sword—but only the wealthiest warriors could afford such a beautiful sword as this one. Parts of the ornate handle are decorated with precious gold and silver.

- The sword was discovered in an unusually large grave. Four post holes around the grave showed it once had a roof. These things tell us the person buried there was very important.

- At the top of the handle is a tiny gold hand holding a Christian cross. The two "X" symbols may stand for the Greek word *Xristos*, which means Christ. The sword was made at a time when the Vikings were turning away from their old gods and goddesses and becoming Christians.

- The long iron blade has rusted and its tip is missing. Bits of leather and wood were found on the blade. These probably came from the sword's protective case, or scabbard.

- Vikings celebrated the strength and sharpness of their swords by giving them impressive names such as Battle-flame or Leg-biter.

- This sword was found in Norway alongside a silver coin from England. The date of the sword is just right for its owner to have fought in England for the Viking king Canute.

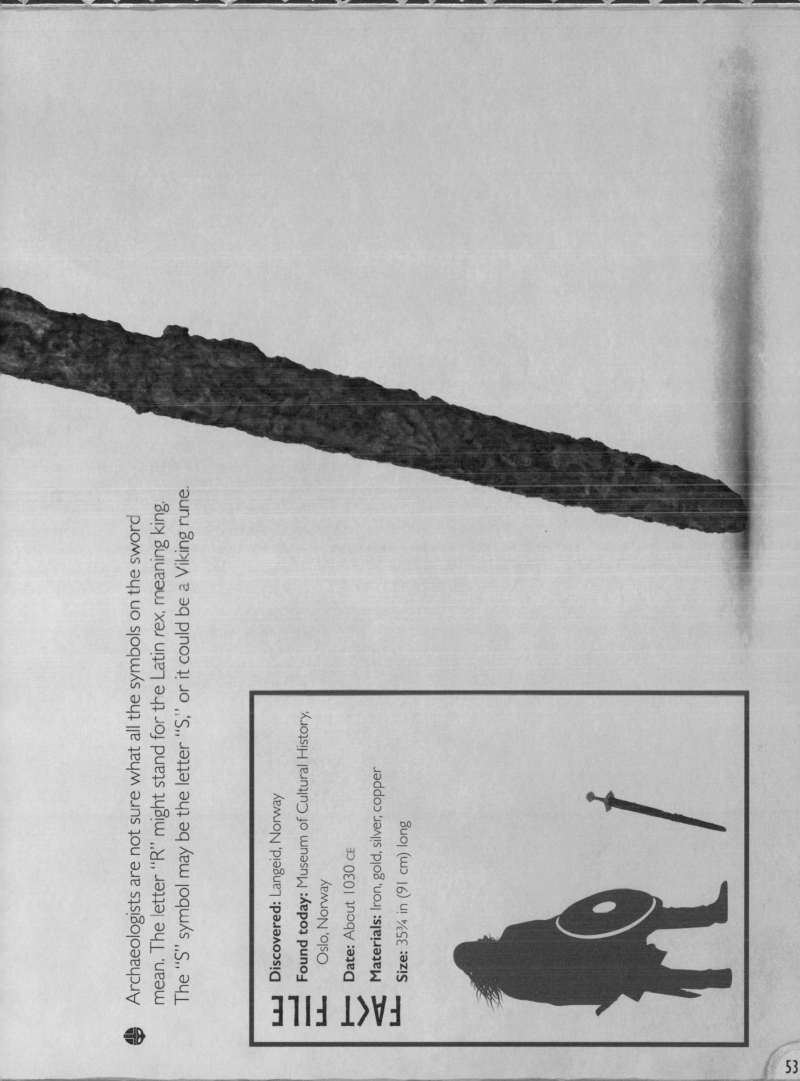

Archaeologists are not sure what all the symbols on the sword mean. The letter "R" might stand for the Latin rex, meaning king. The "S" symbol may be the letter "S," or it could be a Viking rune.

FACT FILE

Discovered: Langeid, Norway

Found today: Museum of Cultural History, Oslo, Norway

Date: About 1030 CE

Materials: Iron, gold, silver, copper

Size: 35¾ in (91 cm) long

THE SILVER HOARD

- These silver coins were part of a treasure hoard that lay buried for more than a thousand years. The owner probably wanted to keep the coins safe, or perhaps they were an offering to the gods.

- Some of these coins have been cut into pieces. For most of the Viking age, the value of a coin was in its weight. Coins and other silver objects could be chopped into smaller pieces and used for trade.

- Some of the coins found in this hoard were from Scandinavia. But most were made in other countries, including Germany and England. A lot of coins came to Scandinavia from trade to the east, selling goods including furs and birds of prey.

- Coins such as these provide useful information. The designs and inscriptions stamped on them help experts to date other objects found in the treasure hoard.

FACT FILE

Discovered: Undrom, Boteå, Ångermanland, Sweden

Found today: Swedish History Museum, Stockholm, Sweden

Date: 800–1100 CE

Materials: Silver

Size: ¾ in (1.8–2 cm) wide, 0.03–0.07 oz (0.8–2 g) weight

- This hoard contained 1,695 coins altogether. It also included a beautiful bracelet and chopped-up "hack" silver.

- In 1999, two silver hoards were found side by side on the Swedish island of Gotland. Between them, they contained 14,000 coins and 500 rings. It was the largest hoard of Viking silver ever discovered.

WINTER BOOT

- This boot is one of a pair discovered in a famous ship burial at Oseberg, Norway. It probably belonged to one of two women found buried on the ship.

- The seams of the boot are on the inside, making it look smooth. The leather was stitched together inside out, and then turned the right way round.

- The boot was designed to keep the foot warm in the snow and ice of winter.

- Leather boots and shoes were usually made from goatskin or calfskin. Leather was also used to make everyday objects, such as bags, pouches, belts, and saddles and bridles for horses.

- In the winter, the Vikings wore woollen socks made from woven cloth. These were wrapped around the leg up to the knee.

- The boot is sewn from many pieces of leather and has a separate sole. The Vikings spent a lot of time on their feet, so their shoes wore through quickly. New soles could be sewn on when they needed replacing.

- Men, women, and children wore similar footwear. Shoes and boots could be slip-ons, or might be fastened with leather ties and toggles. Wealthy people sometimes had colored leather or decorative seams.

FACT FILE

Discovered: Oseberg burial mound, near Tønsberg, Norway

Found today: Viking Ship Museum, Oslo, Norway

Date: 834 CE

Materials: Leather

Size: 9½ in (24 cm) long

THE KING'S CUP

● Fantastic animals twist and turn around this tiny silver cup. Their coiling bodies are patterned with beads. This style of Viking art is known as the Jelling style after the place where the cup was found.

● This richly decorated cup was discovered in the burial chamber of an important Viking, probably that of King Gorm the Old and his wife. The grave was robbed in Viking times and only a few objects were found in the tomb when it was reopened in 1920.

● King Gorm might have drank from this special cup at feasts. Both rich and poor Vikings held feasts to celebrate religious festivals, the coming of summer, and the arrival of harvest time. Musicians played for the guests, while poets called skalds told thrilling tales.

● The Vikings enjoyed drinking beer, made from barley and hops, and mead, a drink made from honey. Wealthy Vikings may have drunk wine or other drinks using expensive glasses from Europe.

● The body of King Gorm was moved after it was buried with this cup. Archaeologists think that Gorm's son, King Harald Bluetooth, reburied it under a church. Harald became a Christian during his reign, so wanted his father to have a Christian burial.

FACT FILE

Discovered: Jelling, Jutland, Denmark

Found today: National Museum of Denmark, Copenhagen, Denmark

Date: 958 CE

Materials: Silver, gilt

Size: 1¾ in (4.3 cm) high

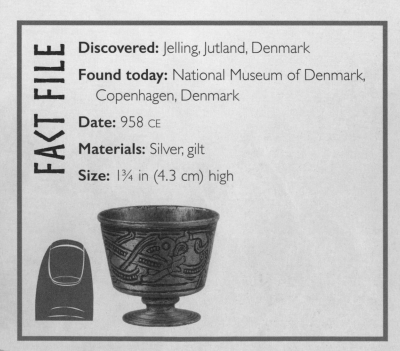

THE CARVED WARRIOR

- A powerful warrior chieftain is shown sitting in his seat. He wears a pointed helmet and is surrounded by his treasured weapons.

- This grave marker was found in northern England. The Vikings first raided the British Isles in 793 CE. Gradually, Viking raiders and traders began to settle in many areas of Britain.

- The stone sculpture was probably created for the local chieftain and landowner.

- The authority of the lord shown on the cross tells us how quickly Christian Vikings settled into Anglo-Saxon England, becoming local lords and landholders there.

- The warrior holds a spear in his right hand. Lightweight spears could be thrown at an enemy from a distance. Heavier spears, with a wide blade, were used for close fighting.

- A large knife called a seax hangs from the warrior's belt. Seaxes were used as both fighting and hunting weapons.

- On the back of the cross is a carving of an animal, which may have been meant to represent a dragon or serpent. These were popular creatures in Viking mythology.

FACT FILE

Discovered: Middleton, UK

Found today: St Andrew's Church, Middleton, UK

Date: 876–954 CE

Materials: Stone

Size: 41¾ in (106 cm)

JUG FOR A FEAST

- This jug was discovered in a wealthy woman's grave. The Vikings believed treasured belongings such as these would be useful in the next world.

- The dark surface of the jug once gleamed with polish. It was probably decorated with strips of tin foil that reflected the light.

- This type of jug is called a Tating jug. Tating is a village in Germany where pottery like this was first discovered. Archaeologists have found several such jugs in the graves of rich and important Vikings.

- The jug was probably used to serve wine at a feast. It was an expensive piece that would have impressed the owner's guests.

- Jugs such as this one are sometimes decorated with tin foil crosses. Some experts believe the jugs were used in the Christian ritual of Holy Communion.

- Most Scandinavian pottery made in Viking times was not as sophisticated as this jug. Layers of clay were shaped and smoothed to make pots, bowls, and jars. In the late Viking age, craftspeople began to use wheels to shape more ornate pottery.

FACT FILE

Discovered: Björkö, Adelsö, Uppland, Sweden

Found today: Swedish History Museum, Stockholm, Sweden

Date: 800–1100 CE

Materials: Ceramic

Size: 9½ in (24 cm) high, 7 in (18 cm) wide

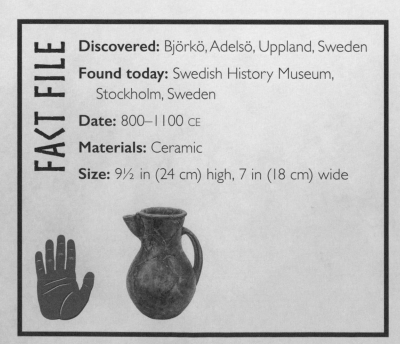

BRONZE KEY

- Carrying a key was a sign of importance and responsibility in Viking times. This small, delicate key was probably used for an ornamental box. The box may have been used to lock away prized objects, such as jewelry or coins.

- Many keys from the Viking age have been discovered in women's graves. In some families, it may have been the job of a woman to look after the household keys. They were often carried on a belt around the waist.

- Stealing was a serious crime to the Vikings. Someone suspected of being a thief might have to take a test, such as picking stones out of boiling water. The Vikings believed the gods would help the innocent, and the test would show who was guilty.

- Most Viking families had a locked chest or box to keep their valuable belongings. The chest was used to store bedding, clothing, and tools.

FACT FILE

Discovered: Borrby, Skåne, Sweden

Found today: Swedish History Museum, Stockholm, Sweden

Date: 793–1066 CE

Materials: Bronze

Size: 2¼ in (6 cm) long

A skilled metalworker designed this key. These artists worked with precious metals, from copper and bronze to gold. They made valuable jewelry as well as everyday objects, such as buckles and keys.

A Norse poem called "Rigsthula" describes a Viking family. The husband is a carpenter, his wife makes clothes, and their son is a farmer. The poem tells us how the son's wife wears clothes made from goatskin and carries a set of keys.

BOX BROOCH

- This glittering brooch belonged to an important Viking woman. She probably used it to fasten her cloak beneath her chin. Both men and women wore cloaks around their shoulders for warmth.

- This type of brooch is called a box brooch. It is shaped like a drum and could also be used as a small container.

- Viking women wore different types of brooches. It was common for them to wear two oval brooches, one on each shoulder. They were used to hold up an "over-dress," which was worn like an apron over a long "under-dress."

- Men fastened their cloaks with a single brooch on one shoulder. A right-handed man chose his right shoulder so that his sword arm was always free.

- Some brooches, such as oval ones, were popular across the Viking world. Others were only found in certain areas. This type of box brooch was fashionable on the Swedish island of Gotland.

FACT FILE

Discovered: Gotland, Sweden

Found today: Swedish History Museum, Stockholm, Sweden

Date: 1000–1100 CE

Materials: Bronze, silver, gold, niello

Size: 3 in (7.5 cm) wide

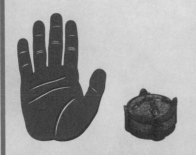

Only the wealthiest Vikings could afford to wear brooches made of gold and silver. Copper and lead were less expensive options.

TRADER'S WEIGHTS

- A Viking merchant used these weights with a pair of scales to weigh silver and coins. This helped make sure they were getting a fair deal.

- Viking traders sold goods including timber, animal furs, iron, and walrus tusks. In exchange, they bought goods such as wheat from the British Isles, pottery and wines from the Mediterranean, and silks and spices from Turkey and Iraq.

- The Vikings didn't produce their own coins until the end of the tenth century. Before that time, they bought goods with chopped-up silver jewelry and coins from other countries. Traders weighed this to find out how much it was worth.

- These weights are stamped with dots, like dice. The dots told the trader how much the different pieces weighed.

FACT FILE

Discovered: Yorkshire, UK

Found today: British Museum, London, UK

Date: About 865–900 CE

Materials: Lead

Size: ¼–½ in (0.6–1.4 cm) high, 0.1 oz (2.58 g) weight

Balance scales had two small bowls that hung from either side of a rod. A trader could weigh silver by putting it in one bowl. The weights were then added to the other bowl until the two sides were balanced.

Some towns became important trading centers for the Vikings. These included Birka in Sweden, Hedeby in Germany, York in England and Kiev in Ukraine. Archaeologists have made many exciting finds in these places.

GOLDEN GODDESS

- This shiny figurine was found buried in a field in Denmark. It was an exciting find because it tells us a lot about Viking women's clothing and jewelry.

- The woman wears an ankle-length dress with long sleeves. The design of the gown is very detailed, with many different patterns. There are scattered lines, grooves, raised squares, and stamped circles.

- The woman's hair is pulled back in a tight bun. A hole between the bun and her ear shows the figurine was worn as a pendant round someone's neck.

- The position of the woman's hands may hint that she is pregnant. Some experts think she represents the Viking fertility goddess Freya. In Viking legends, Freya wore a cloak made from falcon feathers.

- Around the woman's neck is a necklace. The circles may be the rings of a gold chain, or amber or glass beads. Wearing a necklace like this was a sign of wealth and importance.

- The woman's body is flattened but she has a rounded, three-dimensional head. This is very unusual, as most figurines from this period were completely flat.

- There is a brooch between the woman's hands. Similar brooches have been found before, though usually decorating the chest. This figurine shows that they were also worn at the waist, on what may be a belt.

FACT FILE

Discovered: Revninge, Denmark

Found today: Viking Museum Ladby, Kerteminde, Denmark

Date: Around 800 CE

Materials: Silver, gold

Size: 1¾ in (4.6 cm) high

THE BURIED SLEDGE

- This sledge was discovered in the Oseberg burial ship. The rich grave contained the bones of two Viking women and many wonderful treasures.

- The ornate and detailed woodwork suggests that the sledge was not meant for everyday use. It was built for use in ceremonies.

- In the winter, sledges were the best way to carry goods across snow and ice. Overland travel was more difficult in the summer. A wagon couldn't carry as much weight as a sledge, and crossing rivers and lakes was more complicated.

- Horses were used to pull large sledges. Iron studs were nailed to their hooves to stop them from slipping on icy ground.

- Traces of black and red paint were found on the sledge's wood. In Viking times, it looked bright and colorful against the white snow.

- As well as sledges, the Vikings used skis and skates to get around in the winter. Ice skates were made by tying horse bones to the soles of leather boots.

FACT FILE

Discovered: Oseberg burial mound, near Tønsberg, Norway

Found today: Viking Ship Museum, Oslo, Norway

Date: Around 834 CE

Materials: Beechwood, iron, tin

Size: 88½ in (225 cm) long, 17¾ in (45 cm) high, 22¾ 30¾ in (58–78 cm) wide

KING OF THE GODS

- Many experts think this seated figure shows Odin, king of the Viking gods. Odin was the god of war, wisdom, and warriors. His many magical powers included the ability to change into any person or animal.

- Odin sits on his magical throne, known as Hlidskjalf. It gave him the power to gaze into every corner of the Viking universe.

- Two birds perch on the throne. They are believed to be Odin's special ravens, Huginn and Muninn. Their names mean "thought" and "memory." Each day, Odin sent them out into the world so they could tell him what they saw and heard.

- The two animal heads behind Odin are probably his wolves, Geri and Freki. These loyal beasts accompanied their master everywhere.

- Some legends tell of how Odin had one blazing eye. He gave up his other eye for the gift of wisdom.

- The figure wears a long robe and apron, as well as four beaded necklaces. These make some experts think the figure is female. Others believe Odin could be dressed in female clothes. It could also be Odin's wife, Frigg, or the fertility goddess, Freya.

FACT FILE

Discovered: Near Lejre, Sjælland, Denmark

Found today: Roskilde Museum, Roskilde, Denmark

Date: About 900 CE

Materials: Silver

Size: ¾ in (1.75 cm) high, ¾ in (2 cm) wide, ½ in (1.25 cm) deep

ARRIVING AT VALHALLA

- Odin's fabulous horse, Sleipnir, can be seen near the top of this stone. The eight-legged beast carried his master across land, sea, and sky. In this scene, Sleipnir probably bears a rider to Valhalla, the Viking place of the dead.

- The Vikings and their ancestors celebrated brave warriors and glorious battles by making decorated stones like this one. The stones were carved with pictures and with letters called runes, and placed in public places where they could be admired.

- In front of the large horse is a Valkyrie. She holds up a drinking horn to greet the horse's rider. Valkyries carried the souls of fallen warriors to Valhalla. Every evening, Odin feasted with the dead warriors in Valhalla's majestic banquet hall.

- This stone comes from the Swedish island of Gotland. About 450 have been found there. They were brightly colored, though most have faded with age.

- The ship at the bottom of the stone is packed full of armed warriors. It has a large rectangular sail. No complete sails have survived from the Viking age, so experts rely on information from pictures such as this one.

- There are runes running down either side of the stone. They tell us that it was built in memory of the warrior Hjorulf, who died during a Viking raid. The name Hjorulf means "sword wolf."

FACT FILE

Discovered: Tjängvide, Gotland, Sweden

Found today: Swedish History Museum, Stockholm, Sweden

Date: 700–800 CE

Materials: Limestone

Size: 5 ft 8½ in (1.74 m) high

THE CHIEFTAIN'S AXE

This great axe head is one of the most incredible finds from the Viking age. It probably belonged to a rich and powerful chieftain. He would have carried the axe as a sign of his importance.

The Vikings needed axes to build ships, houses, and carts. They also used them as dangerous weapons in battle. Some were small throwing axes, while others were used in vicious hand-to-hand fighting.

This axe is too beautiful to have been used as a weapon. The detailed, swirling pattern is created with silver wires.

The design may show the great ash tree Yggdrasil. Its branches supported the different parts of the Viking universe. At the top was Asgard, the home of the gods, and among its roots was icy Niflheim, the realm of the dead.

Some archaeologists believe the symbols on the axe head are Christian. They think the pattern on this side may be the tree of life from the Garden of Eden. This symbol appears several times in the Bible.

The axe head was found in a richly furnished grave. The man buried there wore expensive clothing. A large wax candle was placed on his coffin.

A fabulous bird appears on the other side of the axe head. It may be the rooster Gullinkambi. Viking myths tell of how he will crow at the beginning of the end of the world—an event called Ragnarök.

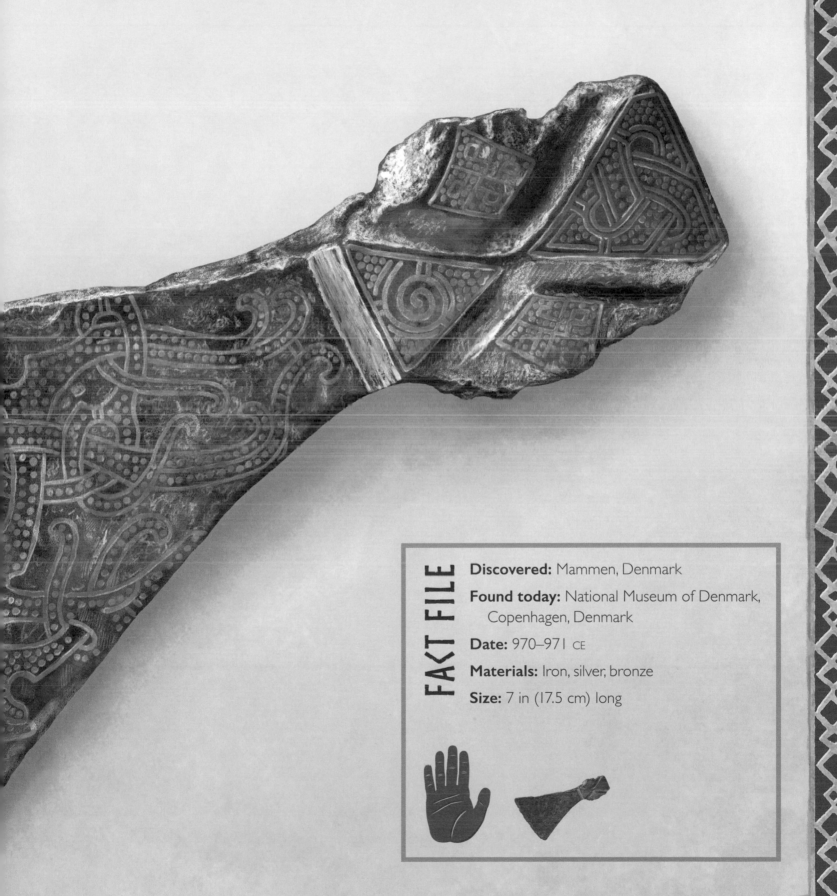

FACT FILE

Discovered: Mammen, Denmark

Found today: National Museum of Denmark, Copenhagen, Denmark

Date: 970–971 CE

Materials: Iron, silver, bronze

Size: 7 in (17.5 cm) long